Take That On The Road

Piers Morgan

Photographs by Philip Ollerenshaw

B▦XTREE

First published in Great Britain in 1994 by Boxtree Ltd, Broadwall House, 21 Broadwall, London SE1 9PL.

Text © 1994 by Piers Morgan. Photographs © Philip Ollerenshaw, c/o Idols Licensing & Publicity Ltd.

Edited by Krystyna Zukowska

Designed by ArtAtac Design

Printed by Cambus Litho Ltd, East Kilbride, Scotland

ISBN: 1 85283 396 3

10 9 8 7 6 5 4 3

A CIP catalogue entry is available upon request from the British Library.

Contents

Howard Donald

Japan was a bit special. It's just such an amazing place. The fans there are really wild and the presents they give you are wild too! Robbie was their favourite, and he was given expensive CD players. I kept going down to the hotel lobby trying to get a CD player because I haven't got one at home. But all I was given was loads of electric razors - I think they were trying to tell me that I needed a shave! I think

Robbie must have said something in one of the Japanese magazines to make sure he got all the good presents. Next time I'm going to make sure I say something about CD players too! They must be the richest fans in the world because they all check into the hotels we stay in. The girls are really determined in Japan.

America was OK, but it was very hard work. Everyone imagines it must have been brilliant, but we had such a tight schedule that we didn't

6

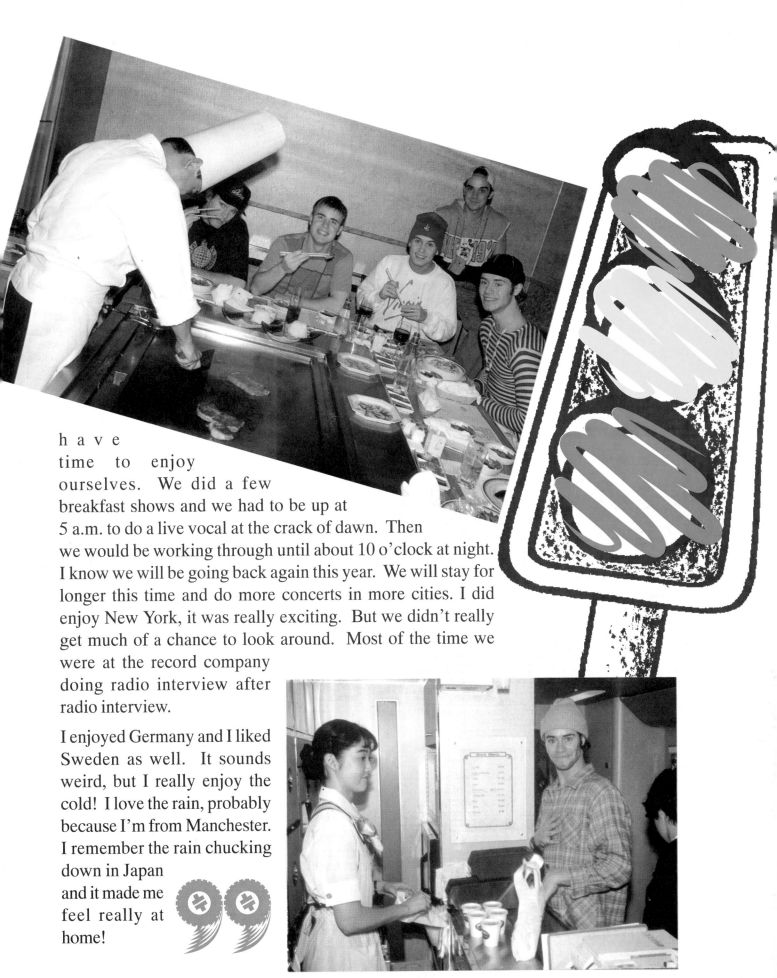

h a v e
time to enjoy
ourselves. We did a few
breakfast shows and we had to be up at
5 a.m. to do a live vocal at the crack of dawn. Then
we would be working through until about 10 o'clock at night.
I know we will be going back again this year. We will stay for
longer this time and do more concerts in more cities. I did
enjoy New York, it was really exciting. But we didn't really
get much of a chance to look around. Most of the time we
were at the record company
doing radio interview after
radio interview.

I enjoyed Germany and I liked
Sweden as well. It sounds
weird, but I really enjoy the
cold! I love the rain, probably
because I'm from Manchester.
I remember the rain chucking
down in Japan
and it made me
feel really at
home!

"It sounds weird, but I really enjoy the cold!"

8

9

JASON ORANGE

"There have been so many great places that we've been to. When the last tour ended I had a break on my own in Mauritius and it was wonderful. I just chilled out, and came back feeling really mellow. I've said many times before that I love Japan. The people are really friendly and they know how to treat their guests. The standard of living there is so high. It's a rich country, and it's so clean. The way we were treated in the hotels and in the recording studios was amazing. They really are a well-mannered race. The Japanese girls were really coy at first - they came across as shy, just giggling and hiding behind their hands. Then after you speak to them for a while, they just open up to you - and *boy* do they open up to you! They just get louder and make loads of noise and then charge at you! They devise plans to get into your hotel. Very rarely do fans get beyond the security measures, but in Japan they always find a way. We've never before had the problem of opening our hotel room doors and finding a fan there, because usually the security guards get there first. But in Japan there's a knock at the door every five minutes from a fan who has sneaked past security. Last year we were doing a signing session outside one of the hotels in Japan and on one side there were thorn bushes separating us from the fans. However there was one mad girl who cut herself severely by running through this big thick thorn bush just to get at us. That was pretty scary. Amsterdam is another place I particularly like. We have done a few TV shows in Amsterdam where it's all gone wrong for us. On one occasion we

were doing a live acapella when one of us started to snigger and then we all got a fit of the giggles. And because you're in another country it can be a bit embarrassing because they don't understand your humour, and the more embarrassing it gets the funnier it becomes until in the end you just can't sing at all! The same thing once happened in Germany on a big TV show and the producers weren't at all amused.

We've also been to Taiwan and met some Taiwanese breakdancers. They were Kamikaze breakdancers. They had just started out and they weren't very good but were very enthusiastic, throwing themselves on the floor and trying head spins. They had a lot of guts but they were well on the way to killing themselves doing those moves. We then went in and showed them some of our moves. As we were a little slicker they were really impressed. It was nice to then be able to teach them a few moves.

" ... we all got a fit of the giggles"

GARY BARLOW

 All the boys will say it, but Japan really was the highlight! I remember one night there when we were about to go on stage. It was just deadly quiet and I turned to the lads and said, "There's no one in this place." I peeped through the curtains and there they all were, just politely filing in row by row. After the show, when we returned to our dressing room via the stage door there were 20 or 30 girls waiting - all screaming - and one of our security guards said, "Shut-up." And they all did! Instant silence! They're so polite...

A few months before the "Everything Changes" album was finished, I was very unsure about America. I've always felt that we were going to make it there, and I feel now that we have a whole bunch of new material that makes it wide open for us. I am really hopeful. When you go to the States and your plane is coming in to land, the buzz you get when you see the

Manhattan skyline is incredible. I have now been back twice and I feel the same emotion every time. When we first went to the States we played some schools, and it was very tough. They didn't know who the hell we were, and most of them were into really hard-core rap. We won them over eventually and got a rapport going, but it did take time. We did one school and it just wasn't working. It took over an hour before they started to warm to us and I said to the boys, "Look, we just can't go on tomorrow and open with 'I Found Heaven' because they just don't like it". So the next time we went on we did a rap thing, where Jason does breakdancing and Howard does his beatbox stuff and that was it, they took to us straight away. We got a couple of the kids who fancied themselves as dancers up on stage and all their mates cheered. However, I don't think we will be doing anything like that again. If we tried to do in America the same sort of school tour we did here, I think that it would take a couple of years to cover all the schools there. It would

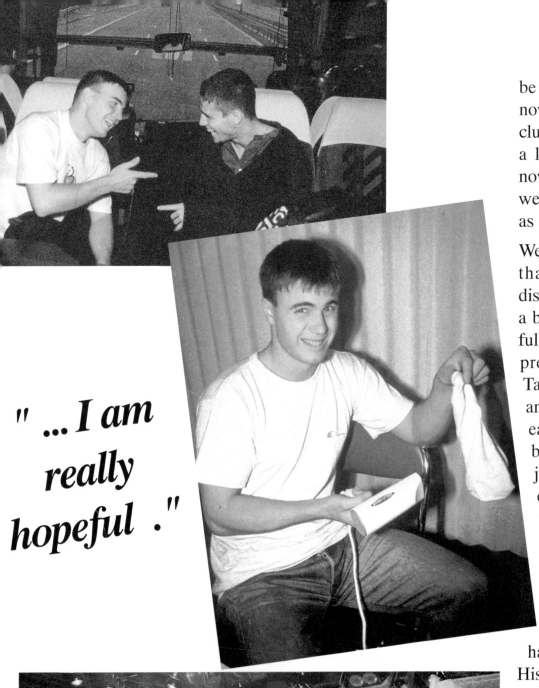

" ... I am really hopeful ."

be really good to get out there now and do some live gigs in clubs and some TV. We've got a lot more under our belts now, a few number ones, and we have established ourselves as a successful band.

We have been to some places that have been really disappointing. Acapulco was a big shock: really dirty and full of beggars. We saw some pretty horrifying things in Taiwan; monkeys in cages and Snake Alley, where they eat snakes. We hadn't even been to Japan then, and we just weren't used to that culture. It was a big shock to the system. None of us had travelled much at all before Take That. Robbie had been to Africa, but the rest of us hadn't been outside of Europe. Jason hadn't been abroad at all. His first foreign trip was to Spain and then that was it - he wanted to learn Spanish! We now call him Pedro - we suspect that on the nights off from the tour he's going around restaurants singing at tables with his guitar! I'd like to visit Australia soon and I really want to see the Taj Mahal in India - it looks so romantic. Finland was lovely. I love all those Northern European countries. Finland is pretty starved of European acts and the fans are always really grateful when you go there. It is weird to go to a country you have never been in, and there are people waiting for you at the airport. A French magazine set up an awards show for us to do there, a bit like the *Smash Hits* awards and we ended up doing a half hour set. It was really good - but very, very cold. Mind you, it was warm compared to Canada - that was bloody freezing! Niagara Falls was amazing. I think one of the best things about being in Take That is that it gives us the chance to visit places like that. We've seen the Grand Canyon when we were in Arizona, and we saw Mount Fiji from an aeroplane. And I loved Hong Kong, which was really quite different. We were taken to a beautiful beach there. I didn't even know Hong Kong had beaches! We have seen a fair bit of the world now, and I'm sure there will be more to come.

MARK OWEN

I loved America. We had a few good laughs there. There's a great little club we went to in New York called Club USA. It's just a dance club, and one of the reasons we go there is because we get in free. But it is really good - and not everybody recognised us there, so we had an excellent time.

I remember the first time we were recognised in the States. We were in a park in New York and Simon Bates was interviewing us - and a girl just walked up to us and said, "Hello lads, what are you doing here?" That was funny.

One of the most exciting things we did in America was appearing on their leading breakfast TV show *"Today"*.

We were only meant to do one number, but because we got on so well they let us play out the show with "Could It be Magic". We are all really hopeful about making it big in America. The first time we went out there was on a promotional tour. I think that is now starting to work as people are beginning to hear about us, we have been featured in a few of the magazines, and on the most recent UK tour a lot of American journalists and TV people came to Wembley to watch us!

While in the States we went to Boston - the home of New Kids on The Block! Stepping off the plane was funny, because we could imagine that a couple of years ago there would have been thousands of girls there waiting for the New Kids to come home. We didn't encounter any hostility from anyone when we were in the States, but we did do a bizarre press conference in Arizona where it must have been about 105 degrees Fahrenheit! We were melting and the questions just didn't stop coming. I suppose all the journalists must have been used to the heat...

Japan is a crazy place. We have been there twice now and it gets better each time. The Japanese record company have really got their act together and it's going amazingly well there. Japan is just like a big electronic city: huge buildings, mono rails, flashing lights. We wandered around a lot there - I think we were dazed by all the lights!

We had some crazy scenes at the hotel in Japan but we were very surprised when we did the concerts. The fans are so polite: when we do a fast number then they all stand up and sing and dance, but when we do a ballad the whole place falls silent and you can hear a pin drop.

Japanese girls are very reserved. If you go to give them a kiss on the cheek, they pull away. But the last time we were there, they got used to us a bit more and came out of their shells. They apologise a lot: when they want your autograph, they say, "Sorry, can I have your autograph, thank you so much, sorry sorry!"

When we first went to Japan, the Japanese security people were so rough that they would push the girls on the floor, but we weren't having that: it doesn't matter that it's a different culture and country - our fans have to be treated properly no matter what country we are in.

Last time we visited Germany we went to Berlin and saw what was left of the Wall. The difference there between east and west was unbelievable. You can see the difference between the cars and the buildings: on one side it will be all modern and the cars are the latest models, and then you look at the other side and everyone has the same cheap car that goes at three miles per hour. It's going to take the eastern side at least 30 or 40 years to catch up.

The people in the east hadn't heard so much about us. We did a couple of radio shows in both the east and west, and many more fans turned out to see us in the west. Germany is a massive pop market and our album "Everything Changes" is doing really well there. I can't wait to tour the whole of Europe.

We have been to most countries in Europe now. Sweden is a lovely place. I had my birthday there and it was snowing, so we had a massive snowball fight. Sweden is really expensive though - it cost us a fortune to call home! More expensive than Sweden was Acapulco, where we shot "Pray". It was really disappointing and I won't be going there for a holiday. It was very dirty with loads of beggars on the streets, which is sad because you imagine Acapulco as this dream-like place. But the beach where we shot the video was great and the people are lovely and friendly. Rob and I had a three hour game of football with some locals, but we couldn't go in the sea because the water is so contaminated. Unfortunately, because we hadn't had any of the injections, when we were shooting the video and got covered in sand and seawater, people just had to keep chucking buckets of clean water over us!

We also had a good time in Paris. The French pop charts are totally different to the British ones. A song can take six months to get to number one there. I think Paris is a very romantic city. We took a boat ride on the Seine, saw Notre Dame and went up the Eiffel Tower. We also tried some French food. I had oysters and they made me sick. I know they are meant to be good for your sex life, but they were horrible! We have now been a few times to Spain. Barcelona is good and really exciting. The very first time we went was just with Nigel and not the record company, so we had a really relaxing time.

ROBBIE WILLIAMS

I know all the guys are saying the same thing, but Japan was one of my favourite places. Holland was pretty good too. Amsterdam is a great place. It's really lively and busy. You can get the best curry in the world there. Everywhere we travel we always take in a curry and in Amsterdam we get the best. Last time we finished our curry there, we went to a bar called "The Bulldog". I did a karaoke number, "Mac the Knife" and got a standing ovation! Nobody knew who I was, but I still got a standing ovation because everyone thought I was good. That was quite flattering; I would have been really upset if nobody had clapped though!

Hong Kong was good fun too! We went there to pick up an award for Best International Band - we've had a few number ones out there: I think that both the English people and the Chinese like us.

When we were in Hong Kong, the guys decided to try lobster

and a waiter came up behind Gary holding a live one. When Gary turned around and saw it he nearly jumped out of his skin - he must have flown about ten feet across the room! It was hysterical, and the lobster did taste v e r y nice - e v e n after the shock!

"I know all the guys are saying the same thing..."

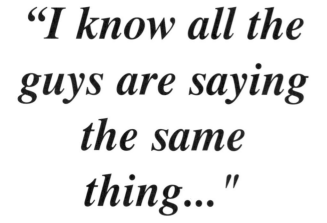

"... but Japan was one of my favourite places"

Howard Donald

"I suppose the worst aspect of fame is the loss of privacy. It took the success of Take That to make me realise that I am a very private person. I know it's part of the job but some of the fans can get a bit carried away. Most of them are very polite and well-behaved when they come to the house, but you do get the odd few who stick their hands through the letterbox, peer through the windows, take pictures of the house and sometimes set the alarm off! I get a bit upset because I know it disturbs my mum.

We do have a big following abroad now. Whenever we do a TV show there is always a really good bunch outside which gets bigger each time we go.

I don't mind at all when I go out and people approach me in the street, but I can't go into town on a Saturday because I just get too freaked out. I tried it once and went with a mate one Saturday morning. I was spotted straight away and before long there was a whole mob trailing me down the street and I just had to make a quick getaway down a side street. It can be quite funny because here you are, surrounded by hundreds of people who all recognise you, but on the other side of the road there can be one old guy asking, "Who the bloody hell's he?"

I don't think I'm as rich as some people think, but I hope I will be one day! I feel really lucky, because although I've always been good at saving up, now if I see something I want, I can buy it without having to save up for weeks. We still pay ourselves £150 a week and the rest of the money is invested. I now know how to invest my money - I'm not daft!

I've spent a lot of money on keyboards and recording equipment. I am hoping to improve my keyboard skills and write more songs. Gary has been doing that for years, and I know it will take loads of practice for me to reach his level. But I feel I am naturally quite musical, so I'll get there some day.

It is difficult to meet people. Sometimes I think I would like to get into a steady relationship because I have had them in the past and it is something I miss. I miss going out with people and you still need to do that, no matter how successful you are.

I would never take advantage of my position. And for me it isn't even a problem because I am just not the sort of guy who could have sex with a fan and then dump her - I couldn't do that. I don't like using people. But we do see loads of attractive girls and I try and get their phone numbers and then store them all up for a later date! But I never seem to get anywhere as none of them fancy me - they're all into Mark or Robbie!

There's no rivalry between us - honestly! We take the mickey out of Mark because he's small, but he's used to that.

I would love to travel more and see as many countries as I can. I can't wait to go to Australia - I think that's on the agenda for this year.

My personal hopes are that all my family remains safe and that if they ever get into any difficulties then I can help

them out. I don't think they will ever change, no matter how much money I may earn or how famous I become - they're all very down to earth and they'll keep me that way too!

"I feel I am naturally quite musical, so I'll get there some day."

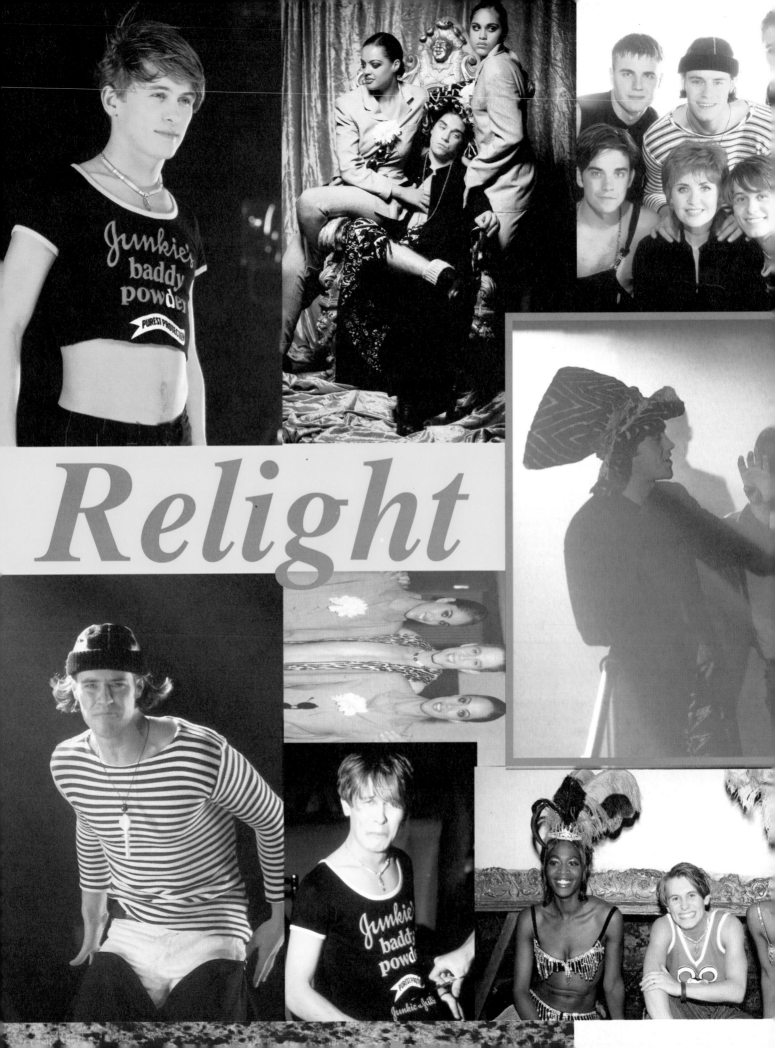

Relight

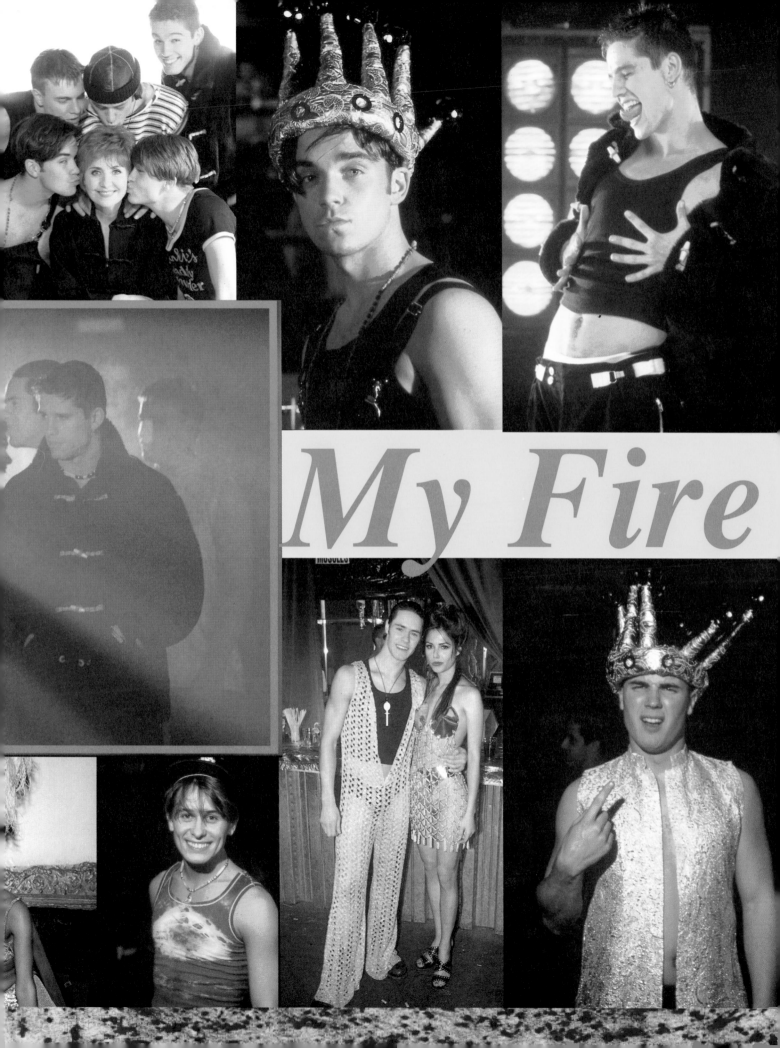

My Fire

"...I don't have a steady girlfriend"

JASON ORANGE

Since joining Take That I haven't really had any dodgy moments. I always try to avoid them. I have been in bars and pubs when you can sense a strange atmosphere building up, but before there has been any confrontation I've always just left. There's generally just the sort of thing that normally goes on in bars; girls approach you and maybe the guys get a bit jealous, but then you leave.

Rob, I know, has a lot of trouble when he goes to watch football. Gary had an unpleasant experience at a service station recently. But I have just managed to avoid all that. And you know what - I think a lot of guys these days tend to like the band!

It's always funny when you visit a new area - a little village or town. You go to their pub or to the shops and the local press always does something on it. It's really nice.

We've been introduced to bands who have been massive and have had number one hits, and when they have been introduced to us, have just frostily said, "We've done it all before, luvvie". I can't stand that! I hope we never turn out like that. I think that they're a bit jealous of our success.

I believe you should try and remain humble the whole time, whether you are achieving success or not. It's more important to be nice to people than to be really famous and unpleasant with it.

We went to the Pet Shop Boys' party last year and that was a real highlight for us, because we don't often go to parties. Sometimes we even avoid showbiz "dos" purposely because we don't want to be seen to be living too much of the high life! But we've met the Pet Shop Boys a few times and they are a good laugh - and they understand the business really well.

We have been lucky with the press so far. They have been pretty positive towards us, and I think that's because we have conducted ourselves well and hopefully that will continue.

It is incredibly difficult to establish any sort of relationship with anybody. I don't have a steady girlfriend at the moment, but in the past it has been very hard to go out

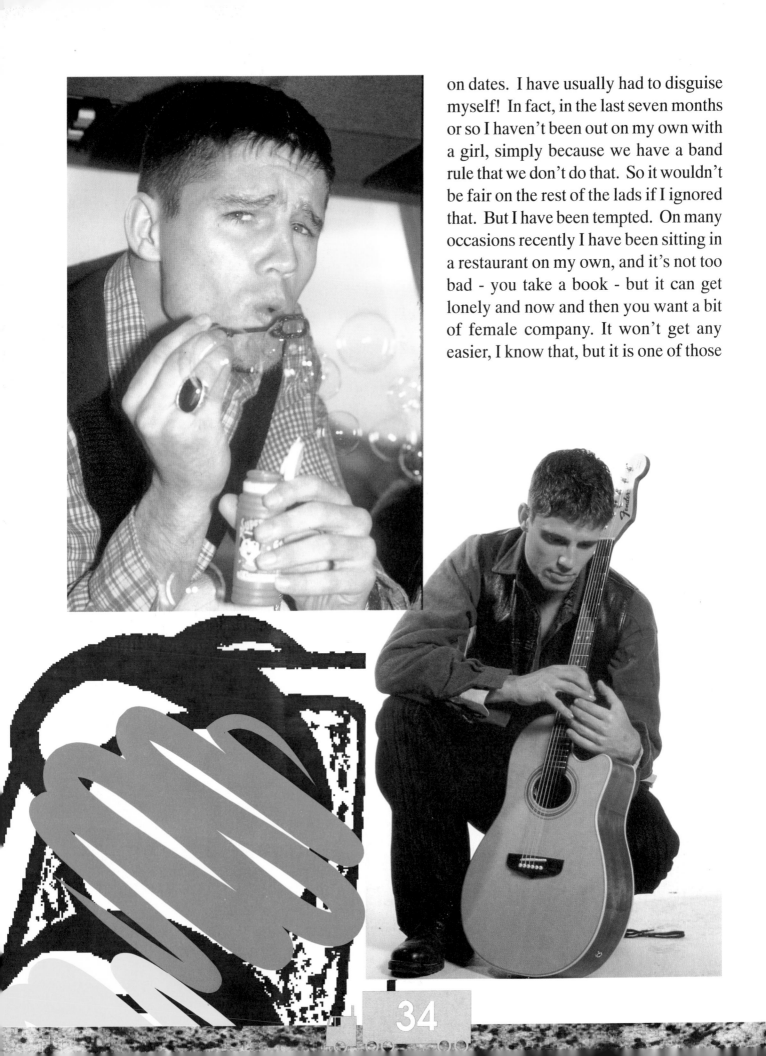

on dates. I have usually had to disguise myself! In fact, in the last seven months or so I haven't been out on my own with a girl, simply because we have a band rule that we don't do that. So it wouldn't be fair on the rest of the lads if I ignored that. But I have been tempted. On many occasions recently I have been sitting in a restaurant on my own, and it's not too bad - you take a book - but it can get lonely and now and then you want a bit of female company. It won't get any easier, I know that, but it is one of those things and we will just have to handle it. Just taking a walk, going to the shops, whatever, you always wish that you could have someone there.

My main ambition for 1994 is to go to Mauritius and not be recognised so that I can spend my time relaxing on the beach! For the band of course it would be great to achieve what we have here in Britain on a worldwide scale. We know it will be tough but we are willing to put the work in and really go for it.

I've decided that on a personal level, this year is going to be a year of self improvement. I'm going to try and be kinder, more caring and more considerate. So those are my personal ambitions for this year and the rest of my life.

GARY BARLOW

 I think we are all pretty worried about the future. The more successful you become, the more weight you carry on your shoulders. People always ask if I get writer's block, but with me every hit we have just stimulates me to write increasingly better songs. I currently have a dictaphone full of new stuff. Howard is getting into the song writing side of things as well. I think it's great that the others are getting more interested in writing new material, because it takes the pressure off me. I had a really good grounding as a musician, working 8 p.m. till 2 a.m. in clubs around Manchester, and because of that it makes me appreciate how much easier it has become. Here we are, going on a luxury coach to do a gig lasting about an hour and a half, and though it feels like hard work, comparitively it isn't. I used to do 36 hours in five days and not earn a quarter of the money.

" ...That was a brilliant buzz! "

Fame is everything I thought it would be - and more. The best part is being able to sit at home knowing that I have created something that everybody in the world will hear.

At the first *"Top of the Pops"* we did, Lionel Ritchie was in the neighbouring dressing room, and as I have been a huge fan of his for years I asked his manager if Lionel would sign a CD I'd bought.

Lionel then came out and introduced himself, and later, as we came out of the studio and saw Lionel and all his entourage coming towards us, he stopped me again and said, "Hey Gary, how's it going!" All the lads just stared at me in disbelief. That was a brilliant buzz!

ROBBIE WILLIAMS

 If I had to say I had regrets these last few months and could go back and change things, then I think I would have remembered Mark and Gary's birthdays! I completely forgot them both. I've just bought Gary a KitKat, but I haven't bought Mark anything yet. I popped round Gary's house and he was opening all these presents and I thought, "You're pretty popular," and he said, "It was my birthday two days ago". Oops!

The worst aspect of our success is the loss of privacy. It somehow just vanishes and you suddenly become public property. Although it doesn't affect me in a big way, it's amazing the number of people who recognise me.

I was in "The Garage" in the King's Road and I was desperate for a pee. I went into the toilet and as it was a bit damp and shady looking, I just wanted to get out really quickly. Then a lad came in and started looking at me oddly, and I thought, "Oh no, he's going to mug me." I then

FAME

finished peeing as quickly as I could and was just leaving when I felt him tap me on the shoulder. My heart stopped and I turned around and he said, "People say I look like you". I was just so relieved that he wasn't going to beat me up!

But I have had people follow me into the loo and ask for an autograph while I was peeing. Someone even asked to have their picture taken with me! I don't think so - not in there, anyway!

I haven't done anything major with my money really. I've bought my mum a few nice things but I don't do that for the publicity. It gives me so much satisfaction to do something nice for my mum, far more than it does to receive anything.

Despite being recognised, I still love going to football matches. I love Port Vale and I still try and get to a lot of the games. It's not too bad; I arrive just before kick off time and go into the sponsor's box afterwards, have a few drinks, sign some autographs and that's cool. I love doing it. I've followed the club all my life.

I've never had much trouble with violence from other

FAME!

blokes because I don't put myself in that position and I'm too fast for them to catch me anyway! A lot of young lads do like us, although they would never tell us to our faces. You can be with a group of lads and they're giving you a bit of stick and then when you get one of them on their own they say, "Actually I really liked 'Babe' " and then ask for your autograph - for their girlfriend, of course!

"*The Big Breakfast*" was a good laugh. I enjoy that sort of atmosphere. It was the perfect vehicle for me. I have now had a few TV offers. I was even offered a part in "*Blossom*", but I couldn't do it because of the tour. We have all been offered adverts. I would love to go and do some presenting, but I just can't fit it in - not at the moment, anyway.

" ...it's amazing the number of people who recognise me."

Babe

Babe

MARK OWEN

Nigel is Take That really. The backbone of our success, the unseen sixth member. At the start he put up a lot of money and took a lot of risks to get us started. He believed in us when nobody else did. Even when family and friends and some of us were starting to give up, he never did. I will always be very thankful and grateful for what he has done.

Although it is incredible to think that all this has happened in just two years, it was a very gradual thing. We started with no fans and then just a few, and a little later a few more and the fame just built up steadily. It wasn't just BANG and there we were.

I love the fame. People do treat you with a little bit of respect when they know who you are. I don't go around demanding it, but when we were in New York, we went to a restaurant and just couldn't get served because we weren't

44

famous enough. The waiters weren't paying attention to us because they were too busy looking out for who might come in next. I would love to go back to that restaurant now and see what sort of service we get! I don't think I'd tip those waiters though. They're there to provide a service - no matter who you are or how famous you are.

The one person outside the Take That entourage I would like to thank is my mum. She has been as important for me as Nigel has been for the band. My mum is so cool about it all, although she still worries about where I am, who I'm with and what I'm doing.

It can be like working on an oil rig sometimes, because you are away so much with virtually no social life. But, obviously, the rewards are fantastic. Better than those on an oil rig anyway!

I want to crack America. That is one of my biggest ambitions, as well as being happy. I don't want to do anything any more that I'm not happy with because life is too short for regrets.

Nigel is giving us more control over what we are doing now. He still keeps the ropes on us but now gives us more scope. We are going to be producing more of our own stuff which will be good. Now we are more established and know more about the business we can take on a bit more responsibility. We do know what direction we want to go in.

We were all really chuffed with the three records that went straight in at number one. I think we are the first band to do that. We were amazed - and absolutely thrilled, of course! I just hope that this success continues. I'm sure it will though, because our fans are so great and loyal and buy all our records just as soon as they are released. We'd be nowhere without our fans.

"...We'd be nowhere without our fans."

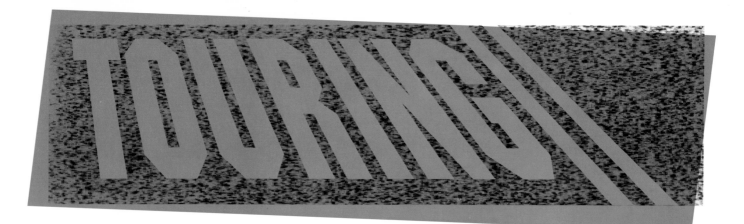

Jason Orange

" We had a couple of outdoor gigs where it all got a bit out of hand - like the big one at Crystal Palace last year. It is scary to see that. We are all very concerned about the fans' safety. We have our minder, James, on the side of the stage and he watches the crowd and if he thinks things are getting out of control, he gives us the nod and we stop the show and ask everyone to move back. It is quite frightening when you see people being carried out because you wonder if they have just fainted or if they are seriously hurt.

The last tour was just brilliant, the third one we had done inside twelve months. On most tours I do have a favourite gig, but on this one every night was a buzz for me. We perform as a band of course, but we all have our individual performances, and

I thought my performance each night was spot on. I was happy.

Manchester is always good because it's the home gig, and Wembley is just amazing. The Wembley shows were particularly exciting because a lot of celebrities turned up. Elton John, Paula Yates, Chris Evans and Kim Wilde were just a few. I love it when celebrities turn up to tell us how much they've enjoyed themselves - I always then have to ring and tell my mum who we've just met!

MARK OWEN

We started rehearsing for this last tour (November-December 1993) about eight weeks ago and we spent the first six weeks at a beautiful little house down south. It was a private house with a recording studio and it was loaned to us by a couple who had a little kid called Jack. At night we'd all sit down and Gaz would play his piano. The lady there used to make Gary sing "A Million Love Songs" to her every night before she went to bed. She said that song and George Michael's "Careless Whisper" were her favourite songs.

We are quite disciplined when touring. We do have a schedule that we try and stick to. We get up at 9 a.m., have breakfast, start work at 10 a.m. and finish at 6 p.m. During that time we'll have lunch. We do get through everything we have to do, but we mess about as well.

For breakfast I'll have poached egg on toast and some orange juice. So we start at 10 a.m, and break about 1 p.m. for lunch. We usually just have sandwiches - tuna is my favourite - and a cup of tea, because Howard can't go without his pot of tea.

When rehearsing, we used to work all day, but we always made sure that we were out of the studio by 7 p.m. We didn't really go out because when you're rehearsing for a big tour, you can't really go out and get drunk every night. We might have the odd glass of red wine with our meal but where we were was so nice we didn't really want to go out that often.

The lady we were staying with used to cook us really big meals - there was always a starter, and as I'm a vegetarian she would make me vegetarian burgers, followed by a hefty pudding like apple pie and custard.

She had a big open fire in the living room, and after dinner we would all sit around that and watch the telly before going to bed.

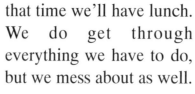
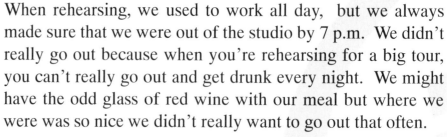

"...we thought we'd be running on stage only half-dressed!"

As rehearsals were progressing we got more and more ideas. For example, we felt "Whatever You Do To Me" was a bit weak, so we thought we would try and toughen the image up by wearing sunglasses, and then we built on that and came up with the gangster idea.

I had the ticking clock idea for "It Only Takes A Minute". We were in a car on the way to London when we made the decision to open with "Another Crack In My Heart". We wanted the opening scene to look like a poster, so that's why we are all doing that frozen pose at the beginning.

Howard first had the idea for a gangster routine because he'd seen *The Blues Brothers*, but there is usually some input from everyone.

We wanted "Pray" to have a haunting feel to it, so that's where the big cloaks idea came from. Gary wrote the music for that when we were in rehearsal. He used my keyboard - which I bought off him for £1000, so that I could practice all my chords, but I've never been on the thing because Gary still uses it all the time!

That's one of the best things about going on stage: knowing that all your ideas are coming to life. The first dress rehearsal for our most recent tour was a disaster. We had a lot of costume changes on this tour and not much time to do them in, but it all came together in the end. Originally we thought we'd be running on stage only half-dressed!

On the day of the first gig, we started about 12 o'clock and had a little rehearsal, then a massage. Jason had pulled his calf muscle, Howard had a bad back. Then a doctor came and gave us vitamin B injections. It just acts as a deterrent against illness and lasts about a month. After the month's up we'll

all drop dead! It gives us a bit of energy as well. Then we came back to the hotel and I had a nap for an hour. We went back to the venue at about 5 p.m. and had some tea. Nigel turned up about 6.30 p.m. and gave us a pep talk and then we went on stage at around 7.30 p.m.

Last time we were on tour our bus only had four beds so we were always fighting over who got to sleep in them. This time we were luckier and we had seven beds, but then only three seats! On any tour I usually go straight to the back seat and put a video on and watch half an hour here and there. It takes about four days to watch a whole film! So far we have watched *Groundhog Day*, *The Bodyguard*, *Ghost*, and *Trespassers* - which Robbie wanted to watch because Ice T and Ice Cube were in it.

We try and get a kip whenever we can. None of us are really that interested in video games. We have a look at what is happening in the papers and magazines. The *Sun* is the first one everyone reaches for.

We all drink honey and lemon to help our voices and keep off colds. We also have to

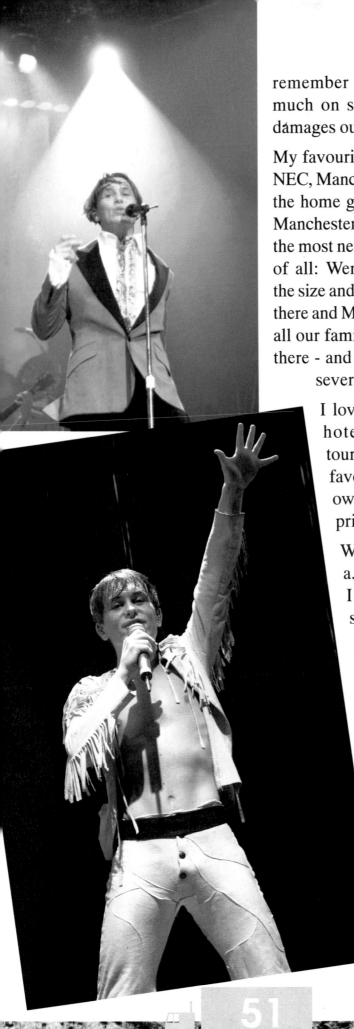

remember not to shout too much on stage in case that damages our voices too.

My favourite venues are The NEC, Manchester because it's the home gig, and Wembley. Manchester and Wembley are the most nerve-wracking gigs of all: Wembley because of the size and all the press being there and Manchester because all our family and friends are there - and they are our most severe critics!

I love staying in posh hotels when we're touring. The Conrad Hotel in London is one of my favourites. The rooms are split so that you get your own bedroom and little living room and it is really private.

When we are on tour I like to get up around 10.30 a.m. and order a big breakfast through room service. I might go for a swim, have a sauna and listen to some music.

I have worked out a lot getting ready for this tour. Rob and I have been doing weights. I went for a run the other day and nearly killed myself. I decided to follow this path that just seemed to go on forever and I ended up in the middle of some motorway! For the next two days, my calf muscles were killing me so I'm not going to do that again in a hurry. But dancing is good exercise as well and we do a lot of that.

We get to the venue at about 4 p.m. and do a whole series of routine things that are necessary for our gigs to run smoothly. Then after 7.30 p.m. nobody can come into the dressing room. I'll usually use that time to have a shower, get changed and do a twenty minute vocal

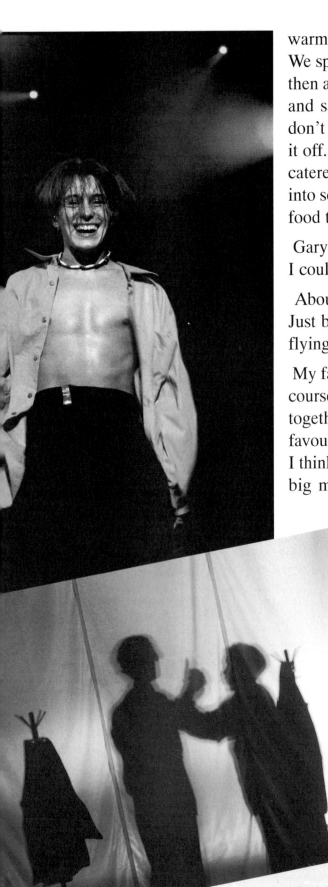

warm up. We make our way to the stage at about 8.20 p.m. We spend five minutes or so soaking up the atmosphere, and then at 8.30 p.m. we get into position. We all hug each other and say, "Have a good one," and then it's showtime. We don't wear stage makeup; there's no point as we'd only sweat it off. We always eat four hours before we go on stage. The caterers do a lot of high energy foods for us but Jason is really into seeds and grains. A lot of what he eats tastes like budgie food to me, but he swears by it.

Gary can fall asleep half an hour before we go on stage, but I couldn't ever do that - I'm much too excited.

About 8.10 p.m. we start getting calls every five minutes. Just before we go on stage, there is a lot of nervous energy flying around - especially on the first night.

My favourite part of this show is the gangster routine, and of course I love the Rock 'n' Roll bit. Jason and Howard jiving together is always brilliant! Jay looks great in a frock! My favourite Take That song is "Why Can't I Wake Up With You". I think that it's such a beautiful song, although "Babe" is my big moment in the show. I was always surprised by the audience's reaction to that. They all knew the song after just one note. It was great having Jason there, playing guitar. He told me afterwards that his hands were shaking so much he thought he wouldn't be able to play. It was a really emotional experience, the hairs were standing up on the back of my neck. I thought I was going to start crying at one point because I could see all the girls in the front row crying! I had to take a deep breath. I didn't want to do a Jacko! I really feel the words when I perform "Babe", but I don't think of one girl in particular. I'm not used to doing solo stuff so I was very nervous at first, but now I really enjoy it.

I love "Pray" and because it is a big favourite with the fans, it's a good one to save for the end. "Relight My Fire" is a good energetic number. We were originally going to have Lulu come on stage with us, but sadly she couldn't make it. We have her on video instead! She sent us some Good Luck flowers for our opening night, which was really nice.

We all made a decision to try and take everything in on this tour - all 25 days. So we made loads of home videos. We also met loads of famous people during this tour. Status Quo were great. Their drummer told us that his daughter has pictures of us all over her bedroom wall. Eric Clapton was nice too; he got our autographs for his daughter.

I would like to have met Madonna, but we couldn't get tickets for her show. The Pet Shop Boys are really great guys. We met them at their party last year and on a couple of occassions since then. We also met

Meatloaf when we did MTV. We were meant to be interviewing him but it turned out to be more like the other way round. We couldn't shut him up! He gave us a lot of advice and was really friendly. He did knock us off the number one slot though, but we'll let him off - this time! But I have to say it is a brilliant r e c o r d , probably my favourite one of the year.

"...Babe *is my big moment in the show."*

HOWARD DONALD

 The last tour was 21 dates. It was absolutely brilliant but it was tough work as well. I don't think the people in the audience realise how hard we work. They just see one show on one night, so they can't know what's gone into that. Even if we weren't doing a live appearance on a certain day, we didn't have that time off because we were doing a press conference or TV show - and we had to make the video for "Babe" as well. Although it was fun, I don't think I could do that again.

We all enjoyed a break after that tour. I didn't go anywhere, I just messed about with my keyboard. I have just bought a new mixing desk, so I am learning to use that. I've been practising on my piano as well.

I know there were press reports claiming that we were all cracking up under the strain, and that's rubbish, though it

did get a bit much for me on the last tour because I caught 'flu and it just drained me. This meant that during the show, when we did the Rock 'n' Roll medley, where I lift Jason I dropped him a few times because I didn't have any strength at all. That lasted through about four dates! He was very bruised at the end of the fourth day...

My personal highlight of the year was "Pray" going to number one. It was just an amazing feeling, and to have it stay at number one for four weeks after that was the icing on the cake.

I know it was a real buzz for Gary because he wrote the song. We were all at home when we heard the news. All my family were crying and we cracked open a few bottles of champagne.

I've got a taste for champagne now - when we go away to foreign countries people always push the boat out and lay on loads of the stuff. None of us drink it though, because you never want to drink alcohol just before you perform. I always try and nick a bottle for later without anyone seeing. At one time I had about six bottles of champagne at home in the wine rack. I never miss a trick!

"...It was absolutely brilliant"

"... and everything was brilliant."

On the last tour, summer 1993, one of the best places for me was Glasgow. The reason I enjoyed Scotland so much was because we hadn't been there enough in the past. When we arrived in Scotland loads of press turned up at the hotel, trying to get pictures and I suddenly thought: This is it, this is what it is all about, this is what people like Elton John experience and here we are going through it. In the early days we used to talk and joke about what it was going to be like when we made it. It is the way we imagined it, but it can be quite frightening as well, knowing that there are people hanging around, waiting for us to put a foot wrong, and always trying to get a bad story on us.

Wembley is very special. Just the word "Wembley" makes me think of all the bands who have played there. I sat in the dressing room and wondered who else had sat in that chair - perhaps George Michael or Madonna!

The first night in Manchester was a horror for me. We did all these rehearsals for months and months. Then we went on stage to do the first number and all that was heard was a piercing noise. I couldn't believe it. Here we were doing our first arena tour, everyone was there, all our home fans, every national newspaper. It was a nightmare, the worst thing that could happen to a singer on stage. I felt like giving up there and then and going home. But then the noise stopped, we started again and everything was brilliant. It did give me a nasty turn though!

We started planning the November/December 1993 tour when we were on the tour bus for the July 1993 tour. Once you are on the road you just want to plan the next tour and imagine what it is going to be like. It is important to start planning as early as possible. The first thing to decide is which numbers we want to do. Usually we sit and write down all

the numbers, and then I go away and put them into some sort of order. The show should always have an explosive beginning, then a bit of entertainment in the middle, and at the end I think you should just go beserk. I basically sort out the running order then I go back to the guys with it and ask them what they think. I always leave the middle section open, because that is our entertainment bit where we put different material in, like the Motown Medley or the Rock 'n' Roll show. There have been about five or six big ideas that we couldn't use on this tour, so we are saving them for the next one. I believe that you have to think, "Right, what are people expecting us to do?" and do the complete opposite - like starting with a ballad rather than a fast number.

On tour, it is so important to get the musical order right - the build up, the ending, playing the hits. We could go on stage and just do every single we've ever released, but the audience would just be bored because they've heard it all before. So the variations, the medleys and the fun, stagey bits are really

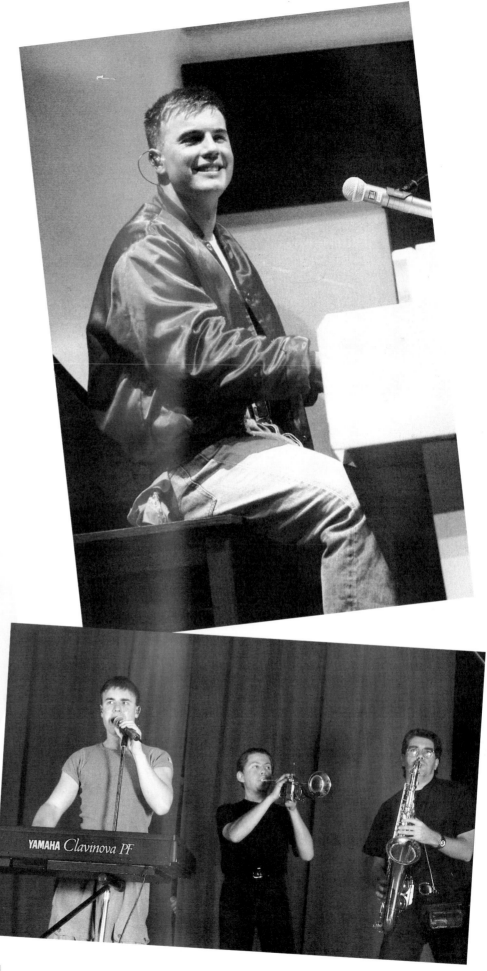

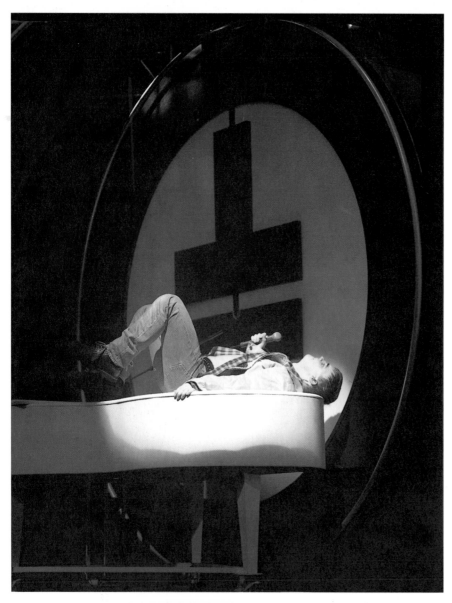

important because they make the show more interesting.

Howard and Jason go away and do all the choreography for the tours and then it comes to final rehearsals. We do work extra hard in rehearsal.

My favourite songs are the newer ones. People don't realise how old some of our material is. "Babe" and "Wasting My Time", were written when I was about sixteen. I like "Love Ain't Here Any More". A big step for me in the future will be to start writing for other artists. But that's a long way off.

On tour we are generally woken about 9 a.m. For breakfast I have Golden Grahams and white toast with marmalade and some mineral water. Then we rehearse. We usually live in at the place

where we rehearse. We all have lunch and dinner together. I'm not too fussed about what I eat, although I'm not a big veggie eater. Jason goes mad at me for not eating enough vegetables, but I'm not showing signs of developing scurvy yet!

This curry situation is getting out of hand. We all love the stuff. I think Korma is my favourite curry or a Masala is pretty good as well. Jason is a real Vindaloo king. I've seen him eat a phal before. I could eat a curry any time, breakfast, lunch, and dinner. I imagine that's not so great when you're kissing a girl!

Once we're on tour it's important to keep the meals pretty light, because of all the bouncing up and down on stage. On tour we will eat at

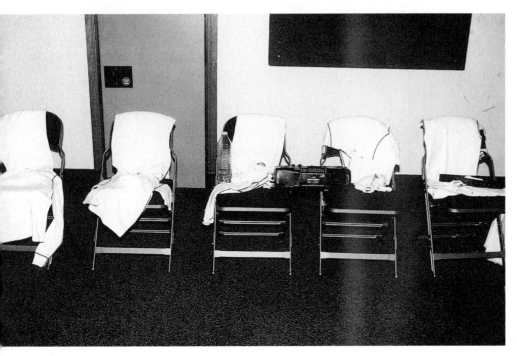

about 4 o'clock, so it's got about four hours to go down. For dinner I usually like soup and bread. On Sunday I do like a roast though: gravy, potatoes and all the trimmings! I haven't recently had much time for one of those!

I don't drink much when I'm working. The odd glass of wine here and there. However, it's Jason who's taken up drinking red wine. He thinks it's good for him because he read in some health book that it stops heart disease and cancer. But not three bottles!

But there again, maybe Jason will live forever now...

It is really difficult to get the food intake balanced because when you are on tour you burn up so much energy. Then you finish and do promotion again for six months, and you still want to eat the same amount, but you're not doing anything, apart from being interviewed all day, so you can put on a lot of weight.

When we're on tour, we all work out to stay in shape. Most days I use the hotel pool, do sit ups, press ups, have saunas, and use the steam room. It's basically just to help me relax and steaming is very good for the voice; it really opens up your throat. Midnight is actually the best time to sing because your throat is really open. It's awful when you do an early morning show like *Live and Kicking* because it's impossible to sing then. So we relax in the morning and then we might have lunch at the hotel or do a press conference .

Then we travel to the venue and check on our clothes. We have dinner at 4.30 p.m. The caterers will cook whatever we want. I'll have soup, a main course and then a yogurt. Then we have a sound check at around 5.30 p.m. We have these ear monitors now and we have to check that they are at the right level with the rest of the band. We then check microphones and just walk around the stage a bit, getting the feel of the place. Stages are all different shapes and sizes and we may have to change some of our moves and entrances, so we run through that as well.

After that we usually do a meet and greet with handicapped children and people in wheelchairs, or people who are terminally ill. We do about an hour's session. Then, between about 7.30 p.m. and 8.30 p.m. we have a little rest and nobody can come near the dressing room. I might have a nap. I suppose you should be really nervous, but I hardly ever am. I can just drop off on the arm of a chair.

Robbie normally tries to put on some rap music, which usually gives me a headache just before I go on stage. We also read all our press. We get all the newspapers and magazines and we go through them. We always read the *Sun*, mainly for the pop pages. Robbie loves his sport and always goes to the back page. I like *Smash Hits*, because you get a good feedback and find out what's going on. I don't like some of the older magazines as I find them a bit pretentious, I would rather read a book. When we are on the tour bus, I just go along with whatever is happening. If Nigel is there, I'll just sit and chat to him.

"...on tour you burn up so much energy."

ROBBIE WILLIAMS

My biggest thrill was "It Only Takes A Minute". The last tour was probably the best time I've ever had in my life and Elton John coming to see us at Wembley made it all even better. That whole tour was one of the highlights for me - apart from one thing, that is. When I was singing "Everything Changes" I went completely off-key and I have never been so embarrassed in my life. I came off stage and I felt so depressed because Elton John had been there and heard me sing off-key. We met him afterwards and I mentioned it and he did say that he'd heard me but that it didn't matter. He is a lovely bloke. He must be one of the biggest stars around and we were really nervous about meeting him, but as soon as he came in the door, the legend was forgotten and he was seemed just like an old mate.

We met him again recently at the Brits Awards. It was brilliant being at that ceremony this February. I think our Beatles medley went down really well as the papers were full of it the following day and people kept coming up to us, telling us how much they enjoyed it. I wonder what the rest of this year has waiting for us - so far it's got off to a pretty good start!

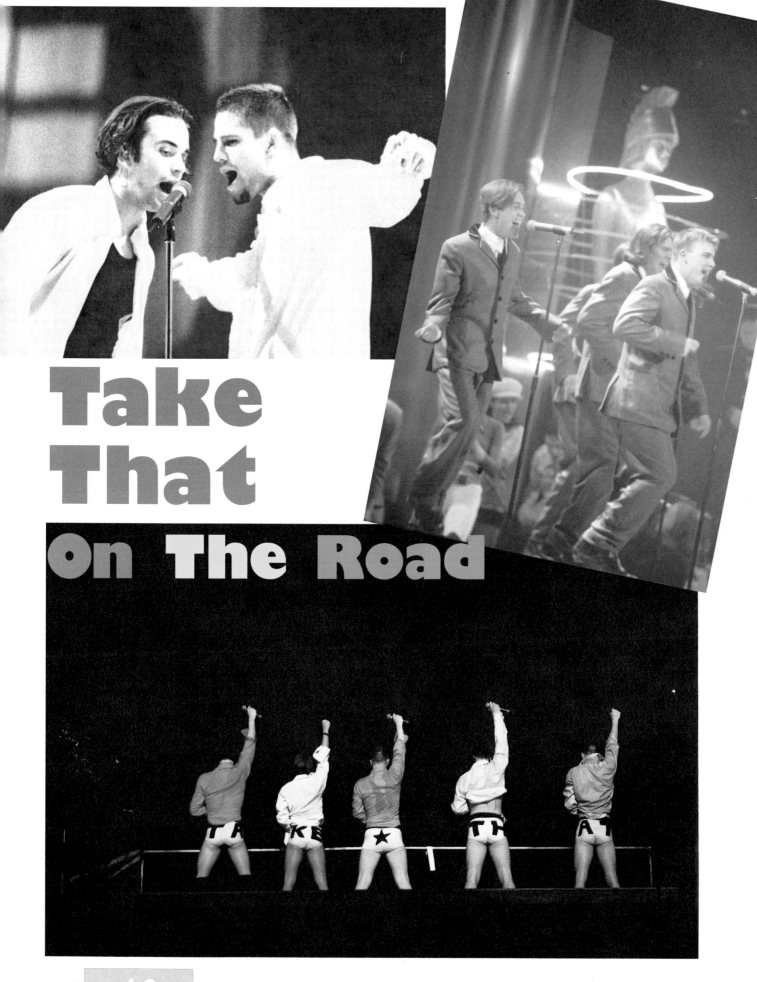

Take That
On The Road

Discography

SINGLES	TITLE	CHART POSITION
July 1991	DO WHAT U LIKE (released on Dance UK)	82
November 1991	PROMISES	38
January 1992	ONCE YOU'VE TASTED LOVE	47
May 1992	IT ONLY TAKES A MINUTE	7
August 1992	I FOUND HEAVEN	15
September 1992	A MILLION LOVE SONGS (THE LOVE SONGS E.P)	7
December 1992	COULD IT BE MAGIC	3
February 1993	WHY CAN'T I WAKE UP WITH YOU	2
July 1993	PRAY	1
September 1993	RELIGHT MY FIRE	1
December 1993	BABE	1
ALBUMS		
August 1992	TAKE THAT AND PARTY	2
October 1993	EVERYTHING CHANGES	1
VIDEO		
December 1992	TAKE THAT AND PARTY	1
November 1993	TAKE THAT-THE PARTY LIVE AT WEMBLEY	1

Fans wishing to join the Take That Fan Club should write for an application form to:

New Members Department
Take That Fan Club
P O Box 538
Manchester M60 2DX